First U.S. edition 1996

Library of Congress Cataloging-in-Publication Data

Williams, Marcia.
The Iliad and the Odyssey / retold and illustrated by Marcia Williams. — 1st U.S. ed.
Summary: Retells these classic Greek myths in a comic strip format characterized
by irreverent humor.
ISBN 0-7636-0053-9
1. Trojan War—Juvenile literature. 2. Odysseus (Greek mythology)—Juvenile literature.
3. Mythology, Greek—Caricatures and cartoons—Juvenile literature.
[1. Trojan War. 2. Odysseus (Greek mythology). 3. Mythology, Greek—Cartoons and comics.
4. Cartoons and comics.]   I. Homer. Iliad.   II. Homer. Odyssey.   III. Title.
BL793.T7W55   1996   883'.01—dc20   96-3588

2 4 6 8 10 9 7 5 3 1

Printed in Hong Kong

This book was typeset in Columbus MT.
The pictures were done in watercolor and pen and ink.

Candlewick Press
2067 Massachusetts Avenue
Cambridge, Massachusetts 02140

THE ILIAD
THE _{AND} ODYSSEY

RETOLD AND ILLUSTRATED BY

MARCIA WILLIAMS

CANDLEWICK PRESS
CAMBRIDGE, MASSACHUSETTS

THE GOLDEN APPLE

In ancient Greece, gods and goddesses lived on Mount Olympus. They watched over human beings and often interfered with their lives.

But when old King Peleus fell in love with Thetis, a sea goddess, she was insulted at being wooed by a mere mortal.

To avoid Peleus, Thetis turned herself into various strange creatures. But Peleus was steadfast and finally Thetis consented to be his wife.

The wedding was very grand. All the gods and goddesses were invited except Eris, goddess of discord, for a wedding should be a happy event.

Incensed by the insult, Eris came anyway, flinging amidst the guests her wedding gift—a golden apple inscribed with the words TO THE FAIREST.

The three greatest goddesses—Hera, Athena, and Aphrodite—each claimed the golden apple as rightfully hers.

The other guests refused to take sides: they were scared of making enemies of two of the goddesses by choosing one.

So the three goddesses returned to Mount Olympus, where they continued their quarrel over the golden apple.

THE JUDGMENT OF PARIS

In time, Peleus and Thetis had a son, whom they named Achilles. Thetis dipped him into the river Styx, hoping to make him invulnerable.

In Troy, Paris was born to King Priam and Queen Hecuba. But he was left to die, as it had been foretold that he would cause Troy to burn.

As luck would have it, Paris was found and nurtured by a shepherd, and he grew up into a fine looking young man.

All this time, the three vain goddesses—Hera, Athena, and Aphrodite—had continued to fight over the golden apple.

One day, upon seeing Paris, they decided he should be their judge.

As Paris watched over his sheep, the three goddesses appeared before him. Tossing him the apple, they asked him to give it to the fairest.

Athena tried to bribe him with the offer of endless wisdom.

Hera tried to bribe him with great wealth and power.

Aphrodite promised him the loveliest wife in all the land.

To Athena's and Hera's fury, Paris gave Aphrodite the golden apple.

Aphrodite was delighted and assured Paris that she would fulfill her pledge.

MENELAUS BECOMES KING OF SPARTA

Aphrodite guided Paris back to Troy, where he was recognized by his parents, King Priam and Queen Hecuba. In their joy, they forgot the prophecy that Paris would cause the burning of Troy and welcomed him home with open arms.

Meanwhile in Sparta, King Tyndareus was trying to choose a husband for his daughter, Helen.

The most powerful kings in Greece were at his court, for Helen was very beautiful.

Odysseus, king of Ithaca, was one suitor, but his kingdom was small and so were his chances.

Seeing Tyndareus hesitate to pick a husband for fear of angering those rejected, Odysseus suggested that Helen herself should choose.

First, each suitor had to swear to defend the marriage unto death. All agreed and fair Helen chose Menelaus, an older but honest man.

For his wisdom, Odysseus was given Helen's cousin Penelope to wed. They returned to Ithaca and grew to love each other dearly.

When King Tyndareus died, Menelaus and Helen ruled Sparta. Helen gave birth to a daughter, and they all lived together contentedly.

PARIS WINS HELEN'S HEART

Back in Troy, Paris was impatient. It was three years after the wedding of Helen and Menelaus before Aphrodite came to fulfill her promise.

Aphrodite had failed to find another mortal as beautiful as Helen, so she urged Paris to cross the Aegean Sea to Sparta.

King Menelaus welcomed Paris and treated him as an honored guest.

But Paris fell in love with Helen and, with Aphrodite's help, won her heart.

One day, while Menelaus was out hunting, the faithless pair set sail for Troy.

Poor Menelaus sent word to his powerful brother, Agamemnon, High King of all the kings of Greece.

Agamemnon sent messengers to Helen's suitors, who had sworn to defend the marriage.

The suitors mustered their soldiers and prepared for battle. From all parts of Greece they gathered on their black ships, ready to follow King Agamemnon to Troy and defend the honor of King Menelaus.

ODYSSEUS FEIGNS MADNESS

Two kings failed to join the gathering armies: one was Odysseus, who was loath to leave Penelope and their son, Telemachus.

When the messengers arrived to summon him, the wily king of Ithaca pretended to be insane and incapable of fighting.

He harnessed the oxen and proceeded to plow erratic furrows through a field.

Then, instead of scattering seed, Odysseus planted salt crystals.

But the messengers were not deceived, for when they lay his baby in a furrow…

Odysseus did not plow him under, as a madman might, but turned the oxen away.

Once discovered, Odysseus relented and readied his warriors and ships.

King Peleus was the second ruler who refused to honor his bond to defend the marriage.

Too old to fight himself, Peleus should have sent his son, Achilles, in his place. But Thetis, his wife, had hidden Achilles.

Having foreseen Achilles' death at Troy, Thetis had disguised him as a maiden and sent him to the palace on the isle of Skyros.

ACHILLES THROWS OFF HIS DISGUISE

Odysseus, swearing to flush out Achilles, followed him to the isle of Skyros.

Discovering that Achilles was hidden in the palace, Odysseus disguised himself as a merchant.

Odysseus then gained permission to show his wares to the royal household.

The royal princesses squealed with delight when they saw his silks and jewels.

But when Odysseus produced a sword, only one hand reached out eagerly.

With a swordsman's grip, the "fair maiden" clasped it. Thus, Achilles gave himself away.

Having thrown off his disguise, Achilles decided he would prefer a short life rather than an ignoble old age. So, with fifty of his father's ships, Achilles—together with Odysseus—joined the fleet setting sail for Troy.

AGAMEMNON ANGERS APOLLO

Landing on the shore below Troy, the armies of Greece made camp.

For nine long years they besieged Troy. Both the Greeks and Trojans were brave fighters and neither was victorious.

The gods on Mount Olympus joined the battle, too. Hera and Athena plotted against the Trojans because Paris, prince of Troy, had given Aphrodite the golden apple. Aphrodite used her powers to help them defeat the Greeks. Then, to make matters worse, the High King, Agamemnon, angered the god Apollo.

To feed his mighty army, Agamemnon had sent raiding parties along the coast.

From one raid, Chryseis, daughter of a priest of Apollo, was kidnapped and made a slave.

Chryseis's father tried to buy her back, but was rudely rebuffed by Agamemnon.

The priest returned home without his beloved daughter. Apollo, who was the god of both healing and sudden death, was so enraged that he sent a plague among the Greeks and one by one they began to die.

ACHILLES LEAVES THE BATTLE

The priest told Agamemnon that only if he returned Chryseis would the plague end.

Reluctantly, Agamemnon told Odysseus to return the maid to her father.

Then, as the mightiest king in Greece, he demanded another slave.

Agamemnon took Achilles' slave from him, the fair Briseis, whom Achilles adored.

Achilles, the most feared of all soldiers, was so angry that he withdrew his army.

Thetis, seeing her son's sorrow, begged Zeus to turn the war against Agamemnon.

So by the power of Zeus, king of the gods, the war began to go against the Greeks. A Trojan victory seemed close at hand.

The Greeks needed the strength of Achilles to hold back the Trojan army, but he was still too bitter and sat brooding in his tent.

From the walls of Troy, fair Helen looked upon the blood-stained plain and regretted the day she left good King Menelaus.

THE ARMOR OF ACHILLES

With the courage of Zeus in their hearts, the Trojans fought even more fiercely. Each day brought them a new victory, and gradually the dispirited Greeks were being driven back to their ships and closer to final defeat.

From within his tent, Achilles could hear the sound of clashing swords, but still he refused to help. So, Patroclus, his brother-in-arms, asked to lead Achilles' soldiers into battle wearing Achilles' armor, which he knew would strike dread into the Trojans.

Achilles feared for his best friend's life, but finally agreed, insisting that Patroclus ride into battle in his chariot.

Achilles watched from his ship with a terrible sense of foreboding as Patroclus led his army toward the Trojan forces.

Seeing Achilles' chariot and glistening armor and believing that he had returned to the fray, the Trojans became scared, and Patroclus and his men soon drove them from the beaches. Many brave Trojan allies were killed, including Sarpedon, a son of Zeus.

THE REVENGE OF ZEUS

Zeus, savage in his revenge, drove Patroclus into the thickest part of the conflict.

Apollo then made Patroclus's helmet fall from his head and his hair blow into his eyes. In this moment of confusion, Hector, second son of the Trojan king, Priam, speared Patroclus through the stomach, killing him instantly.

Then, according to the custom, Hector took Achilles' armor.

In agony Achilles watched all this from his ship. When his chariot returned with the dead body of his dearest friend, Achilles swore to avenge his death.

Agamemnon was delighted that Achilles was ready to fight again and to encourage him, Agamemnon returned Briseis, loaded with gifts.

But Thetis prevailed upon her son to wait until Hephaestus, armorer to the gods, had made him fine new armor.

SCAMANDER THE RIVER GOD

As soon as Hephaestus brought Achilles his new armor, he mounted his chariot and with a ferocious cry led the Greeks into battle. The gods on Mount Olympus heard his yell. The goddesses Hera and Athena instilled fresh courage into the Greek soldiers.

Achilles watched for Hector, the Trojan prince who had killed Patroclus.

Hector lay low, until Achilles killed his brother, Polydorus.

Hector then attacked Achilles. But his spear was blown off course by Athena.

Achilles threw his spear. But Apollo drew Hector into a mist to safety.

His revenge thwarted, Achilles rampaged through the Trojans until the river ran red.

Angrily, Scamander, the river god, told Achilles to cease killing the Trojans.

When Achilles refused, Scamander bid the river to rise up and drown him.

The river rose higher and higher around Achilles until his heavy armor began to drag him under. Seeing his plight, the armorer, Hephaestus, came to his rescue by driving back the river with a wall of fire.

THE DEATH OF HECTOR

Still weighed down by the river water, Achilles once more charged after the retreating Trojans. As he did so, Hector appeared from out of the mist. Achilles lunged at him but Hector took fright and ran off.

Three times they circled the city walls before the gods took the fear from Hector and he turned to face Achilles.

But Hector was wearing Achilles' old armor and Achilles, knowing its weak spot, soon took his chance and stabbed poor Hector to death.

Achilles had avenged his dear friend Patroclus and returned to camp well pleased.

After Hector's death, the Greeks continually drove the Trojans back against their city walls.

One day, cowering behind the gates, Paris spied Achilles and, aided by Apollo, shot at him.

Achilles was hit in the heel that his mother had held as she plunged him into the river Styx.

The horrified Greeks quickly avenged their hero's death by killing Paris.

Without Achilles, the war had to be won by cunning. So Odysseus devised a plan.

THE TROJAN HORSE

Under the guidance of Odysseus, the Greeks built a huge wooden horse and set it outside the gates of Troy. Then, boarding their ships, they sailed away into the distance.

TROY BURNS

The Trojans were amazed and sent out scouts to make sure that all the Greeks had left. One Greek was found, Sinon, who convinced King Priam that the horse, like himself, had been left as an offering to Athena for a safe journey home. So, as the Greeks had hoped, the Trojans pulled the horse into the city square and all day they celebrated beneath this symbol of their victory— while Helen wept for the many deaths she had caused by her faithlessness.

Later, as Troy lay sleeping, Sinon climbed the ramparts with a torch. Waving it high, he saw an answering signal from the returning Greek ships. Then he released Odysseus and a band of soldiers hidden in the belly of the wooden horse. Before any alarm could be sounded, Odysseus had captured the palace and killed the king. The Greek warriors from the ships swept through the city, looting and burning, until all of Troy was in flames.

Only Helen was saved. Odysseus took her to King Menelaus who, because of his great love for her, forgave all. After ten long years, his honor was restored and the Greeks set sail for home.

THE CICONES

The Greeks' return journey was fraught with danger. Pursued by Aphrodite's vengeance, many soldiers were lost at sea.

King Agamemnon guided his ships safely home, as did King Menelaus, who lived in happiness with Queen Helen ever after.

Odysseus, who longed to be reunited with Penelope, was not so lucky. He set out from Troy with twelve ships, each with sixty men on board. Several days out from Troy, the wind blew them to Ismarus, a city in Thrace, where the warring Cicones lived.

Odysseus and his men plundered the city, killing many people.

Then they celebrated their triumph with a party on the beach.

The Cicones went for help and at dawn they attacked the sleeping Greeks.

All through the day the battle raged. Only as the sun set did Odysseus manage to put his ships to sea. But he left six warriors from each ship dead upon the beach. So began the Odyssey, the story of Odysseus' adventurous journey home.

THE LOTUS-EATERS

For nine days Zeus sent winds to toss Odysseus's ships across the rough sea.

Then they reached the land of the Lotus-Eaters and two men were sent to look for food.

Happening upon a sunny glade, the two Greeks came across the Lotus-Eaters, who gave them the delicious honeyed plant to eat. The taste of lotus blossoms drove all thoughts of duty and home from their minds and they relaxed contentedly in the sunshine.

Odysseus had to go in search of his companions and use force to return them to their ships.

Still they would have swum ashore had Odysseus not shackled them in irons.

THE CYCLOPS, POLYPHEMUS

On and on sailed the black ships of Odysseus toward their home in Ithaca until, floundering in thick fog, they came upon the land of the Cyclopes—fearsome giants who had only one eye.

Taking twelve soldiers and a good supply of wine, Odysseus went in search of food. In a nearby cave, the party found a store of cheeses, which they loaded into sacks, only to find their exit blocked by Polyphemus, a giant Cyclops. After herding his huge sheep into the cave, Polyphemus rolled a great boulder over the entrance. Then, with a glint in his one eye, he seized a handful of terrified soldiers and stuffed them into his mouth with relish.

The next morning the greedy giant Polyphemus ate two more Greek soldiers.

Then he left to graze his sheep, having first secured the entrance with a vast rock.

Looking around for a weapon, Odysseus took the giant's staff and sharpened one end.

When Polyphemus returned that evening, Odysseus offered him their wine.

Although it was enough for twelve men, the Cyclops drank it all in one gulp.

Polyphemus asked whom he should thank and Odysseus replied, "My name is nobody."

"Then I will eat Nobody last," cried Polyphemus, and fell into a drunken stupor.

At once, Odysseus took up the sharpened staff and drove it deep into the Cyclops's eye.

So fearful were Polyphemus's screams that his neighbors rushed to the cave's entrance.

From behind the boulder they asked who was killing their friend.

But when the Cyclops cried, "The treachery of Nobody," his friends left.

Stumbling outside, Polyphemus waited to catch his enemies as they made their getaway.

But each man clung to the belly of a sheep and so escaped detection by the blinded giant.

Hurrying to join their ships, the Greeks set sail just as the Cyclops realized they'd gone.

Polyphemus called on Poseidon, his father and god of the sea, and on his uncle Zeus, to wreak revenge.

THE SILVER THREAD

It was with great relief that Odysseus's fleet reached the floating isle of Aeolia.

Aeolus lived there, a kindly man who cared for the soldiers for a whole month.

When they took their leave, Aeolus gave Odysseus a patterned bag tied with silver thread.

Odysseus guarded the bag carefully, both day and night.

After nine days' sailing, the crew sighted their homeland, Ithaca.

Odysseus was so relieved to be nearly home, he fell asleep.

His crew decided to steal the treasure they believed to be in the bag.

So, while Odysseus slept, they untied the silver thread. But it was not treasure they released—it was the howling winds that Aeolus had secured for their safety. A mighty tempest whipped up around the ships, driving them far from Ithaca.

Soon the whole fleet was blown back to the Aeolian Isle. Odysseus asked Aeolus to secure the winds again, but he refused to help a second time and the travelers resumed their voyage in gloomy spirits.

THE HARBOR AT TELEPYLUS

For six days the fleet forged bleakly ahead, until it reached the settlement of Telepylus.

All the ships sailed through the narrow mouth of the harbor . . .

all except Odysseus, who anchored his ship outside.

He sent three men inland for news of the local inhabitants.

They found a young girl who took them to the local chief.

The chief, who was a cannibal, grabbed a soldier.

The other two escaped and ran for the harbor.

But the chief sent his men chasing after them.

The cannibals started pelting the ships with rocks. For the flotilla trapped in the harbor, there was no escape: the ships were cracked asunder and the men harpooned like fish. Only Odysseus and his crew escaped the slaughter.

CIRCE THE ENCHANTRESS

With no wind to help them, Odysseus's men rowed on until they reached Acaea.

For two days and two nights they lay exhausted on the beach.

Then Odysseus went hunting and killed a fine stag.

The roasting meat brought hope back to his men,

and they sent out a party to search for more food.

In time, these men came to the house of Circe, a formidable enchantress. Prowling around were the strangest wolves and lions.

Hearing men approach, Circe opened her door. All but their leader, Eurylochus, went in.

Circe served her guests wine spiced with a powerful drug. Then, when they had been rendered helpless, she struck them with her wand, turning them into swine.

Circe then drove the unfortunate soldiers into sties where she left them to wallow in the mud and to grow fat on acorns—ready to be served at her table.

Eurylochus returned to Odysseus with this bad news.

Odysseus buckled on his sword and made haste for Circe's home. As he drew close, the god Hermes appeared before him. Hermes gave Odysseus some of the magic plant called Moly, an antidote to Circe's potent drug.

So, when Circe gave Odysseus her evil potion it had no effect on him.

Circe tried to touch him with her wand, but Odysseus lunged at her with his sword.

Circe, unused to being outwitted, fell crying to the floor, swearing never to do Odysseus harm.

To prove her sincerity, Circe went to the sties and returned Odysseus's companions to their human form . . .

and also the wolves and lions that fawned around her, for they too were men transformed by her evil magic.

So kind did Circe become that she charmed Odysseus and his men into staying with her for a year before they finally began to yearn for their friends and family at home in Ithaca. Although she knew she would miss them, she agreed to help them on their way.

Before allowing Odysseus to embark for Ithaca, Circe insisted he visit Hades, the land of the dead. Odysseus was frightened, as Hades was a dangerous place for the living and difficult to find, but Circe promised Odysseus her protection and sent the north wind to guide his ship.

In Hades, Odysseus saw the souls of friends killed at Troy and that of his mother, who had died pining for his return.

Odysseus also met Tiresias, a blind prophet, who told him how to overcome future hazards, including the spell cast by the Sirens' song.

When Odysseus returned to Circe, she loaded his ship with food and sent him on his way, reminding him first of Tiresias's warning about the terrible Sirens—the creatures who lured sailors to death upon the rocks by mesmerizing them with their song.

Aware of the danger facing him, Odysseus blocked the ears of his crew with softened beeswax. Then, as they neared the Sirens' rocky isle, three men tied Odysseus to the mast so he would not be tempted to turn the ship toward their song, and certain death.

Although it was said that only three Sirens lived on the rock, it suddenly seemed to Odysseus that the whole sky was filled with the strange creatures and their alluring song. The deafened crew had to restrain Odysseus from breaking his bonds and turning the ship toward their lethal island.

SCYLLA THE MONSTER

No sooner had the danger of the Sirens passed than the crew approached another: two great rocks, little more than a boat's width apart. One rock was the home of Scylla, a dreadful monster with six heads. Under the second lived Charybdis who, by sucking up the sea and spewing it out again, wrecked any ship that chanced near. Odysseus urged his men to row with all speed, keeping close to Scylla's rock.

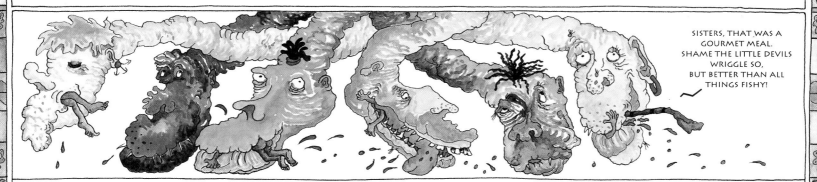

SISTERS, THAT WAS A GOURMET MEAL. SHAME THE LITTLE DEVILS WRIGGLE SO, BUT BETTER THAN ALL THINGS FISHY!

Odysseus tried to fight Scylla off but she was too quick for him. While he mounted the prow, Scylla's six heads flashed down and swallowed a man each. The rest of the crew, though sick at heart for their companions' fate, rowed furiously on.

HYPERION'S CATTLE

Not far from the two great rocks lay the island of the sun god, Hyperion. Odysseus ordered his crew to keep rowing, for he knew danger lurked there.

But the crew was tired and swore not to disturb Hyperion's sacred cattle grazing there, so Odysseus allowed his men ashore.

During the night, Zeus sent a fearful storm. For a whole month the seas raged and the ship was unable to continue its journey. Nearly all Circe's food had been eaten and it was impossible to fish in the storm-tossed sea. The men were dreadfully hungry.

Odysseus went off alone to pray to the gods for salvation.

Eurylochus pressed his friends to feast upon the god Hyperion's sacred cattle.

Close to starvation, they agreed; and soon the aroma of roasting meat reached Odysseus.

Odysseus called upon Zeus to forgive his men. But louder still were Hyperion's pleas to Zeus for vengeance, and Zeus, already angry with the Greeks, listened only to Hyperion.

When the storm abated and Odysseus set sail again, Zeus hit the ship with a tornado, which snapped the mast and tossed men overboard.

Then in his anger, Zeus sent a thunderbolt, which filled the ship with sulfur and killed the remaining crew.

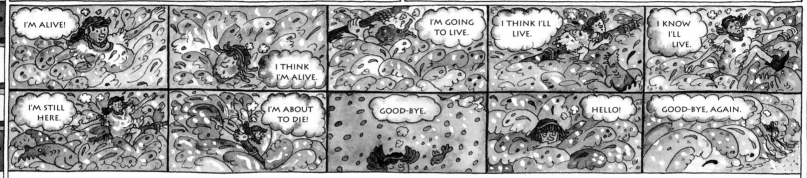

I'M ALIVE!

I THINK I'M ALIVE.

I'M GOING TO LIVE.

I THINK I'LL LIVE.

I KNOW I'LL LIVE.

I'M STILL HERE.

I'M ABOUT TO DIE!

GOOD-BYE.

HELLO!

GOOD-BYE, AGAIN.

Only Odysseus, who had not eaten Hyperion's sacred cattle, was saved. For nine days he was tossed upon the waves. On the tenth day he was washed up on the isle of Ogygia, home of the lonely goddess Calypso. Barely conscious, Odysseus lay on the sand unable to move.

COMPANY, AT LAST.

ISN'T HE A GORGEOUS HUNK?

OOH, I COULD EAT YOU.

Walking along the beach, Calypso found the half-drowned and starving Odysseus.

She took him into her cavern, where she treated him with magic potions.

As Calypso nursed Odysseus, she grew to love him devotedly.

YOU'RE CUTE.

BUT NOT AS CUTE AS PENELOPE?

SHE'S ESPECIALLY CUTE.

I CAN MAKE YOU IMMORTAL.

IMMORTALITY DOESN'T BRING HAPPINESS.

AND PENELOPE DOES, I SUPPOSE?

FOR ME, YES.

WELL, THAT'S JUST TOO BAD.

Odysseus liked Calypso well enough, for she was charming and kind, but he yearned for Ithaca, his wife Penelope and their son, who had now grown to manhood. Yet for seven years Calypso kept Odysseus with her by refusing to let him build a boat.

Athena finally took pity on Odysseus, pleading to Zeus on his behalf.

Relenting, Zeus sent Hermes with an order for Calypso to help Odysseus leave for Ithaca.

Calypso was upset by Zeus's command, but dared not disobey the king of the gods.

Reluctantly, Calypso gave Odysseus an ax and helped him build a raft.

So, in spite of Calypso's immortal tears, Odysseus went to sea once more.

Days later, Odysseus spied land, but just then Poseidon (the blind Cyclops's father) saw him.

Poseidon lifted a wave, engulfing the raft and sucking Odysseus downward.

Held under by his clothes, Odysseus would have drowned if Ino, a sea nymph, had not seen him.

She bid him to undress and swim for the shore of Scheria, with her magic scarf to aid him.

After two days, Odysseus reached land, only to find cliffs too steep to climb.

Seeing his difficulty, Ino sent a wave that washed him onto the bank of a river.

Thankfully, Odysseus flung his savior's scarf back to her in the ocean's depths.

THE PRINCESS NAUSICAA

Odysseus spent the night naked and shivering in a tangled thicket.

The next morning Princess Nausicaa came to the river with her maids to wash clothes.

Odysseus looked out, but his salt-encrusted body frightened away all but Nausicaa.

The princess took pity on Odysseus and bade her maids wash and dress him.

Then she took Odysseus to the palace, where he was promised a safe passage home.

A feast was held in Odysseus's honor, with games and gifts from all the guests.

Early the next morning, Odysseus and his gifts were borne on board a ship and rowed toward Ithaca by the brave citizens of Scheria, who were the finest of sailors. All that day and on through the night and the next morning, Odysseus slept, exhausted by his many adventures.

When Ithaca was reached, his companions wrapped Odysseus in blankets and left him on a beach, surrounded by his gifts.

But Poseidon saw the ship carrying his enemy reach Ithaca. In his anger he turned the vessel and all aboard her into a great black rock.

ATHENA HELPS ODYSSEUS

Although Odysseus had now reached Ithaca, his troubles were not over. During the years of his absence, suitors for Penelope's hand had helped themselves to his house and food. Penelope and Telemachus, their son, had been unable to rid themselves of these unwelcome guests.

Penelope, certain Odysseus would return, told the suitors she must weave a shroud for Odysseus's elderly father before choosing between them.

Each day she sat and wove her cloth, and every night she unraveled it so the cloth was never finished and the suitors had to wait.

Now Athena came to wake Odysseus and warn him of those who misused his home and wished him dead.

After helping Odysseus to hide his treasures, Athena guided him, disguised as a beggar, to Eumaeus, a loyal palace swineherd.

Eumaeus treated Odysseus kindly until Telemachus, who had been away seeking Odysseus, returned.

Athena transformed Odysseus to his former glory and father and son rejoiced at their reunion.

Together with Athena's help, they hatched a plot to rid their home of its hated guests.

THE HOMECOMING

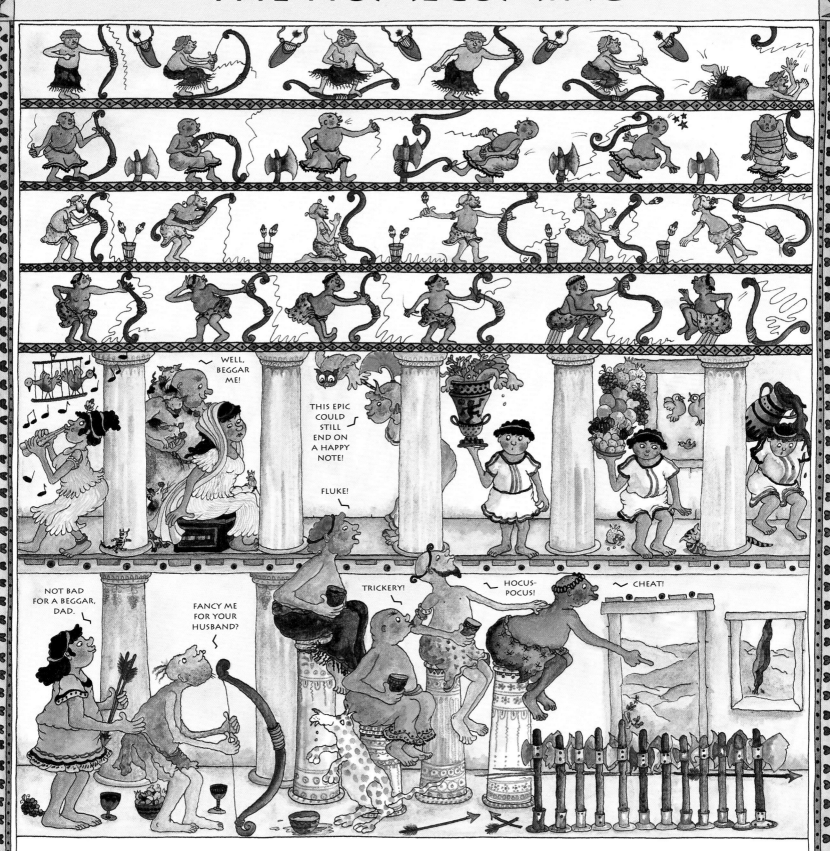

Telemachus went home, inviting the greedy suitors to join him in a feast to which Odysseus, dressed once more as a pauper, came to beg for food. When all had eaten, Penelope, who had not recognized her husband, guided by Athena, brought out his bow. She said she would marry the suitor who could string the bow and shoot through twelve axes, as Odysseus once had. All tried and failed, for it was a mighty bow. Then the beggar demanded his right to try and, amidst jeers, took up the bow. Stringing it with ease, he shot through all twelve axes.

While the feasters sat stunned, Odysseus took another arrow and shot a suitor. Instantly the other suitors scattered in all directions. Athena took off Odysseus's disguise and those who had remained loyal to their king ran to his aid, as did Eumaeus and Telemachus. They drove the suitors from the palace and Odysseus once again took possession of his kingdom and was reunited with his beloved wife, Penelope.

Then Zeus, tired of the warfare that had surrounded Odysseus for twenty years, let fly a flaming bolt, and Athena cried out that the time for peace had come to Ithaca. While stories of the Trojan War and Odysseus's eventful journey home spread across the world, King Odysseus and his loyal Queen Penelope ruled Ithaca wisely and happily.

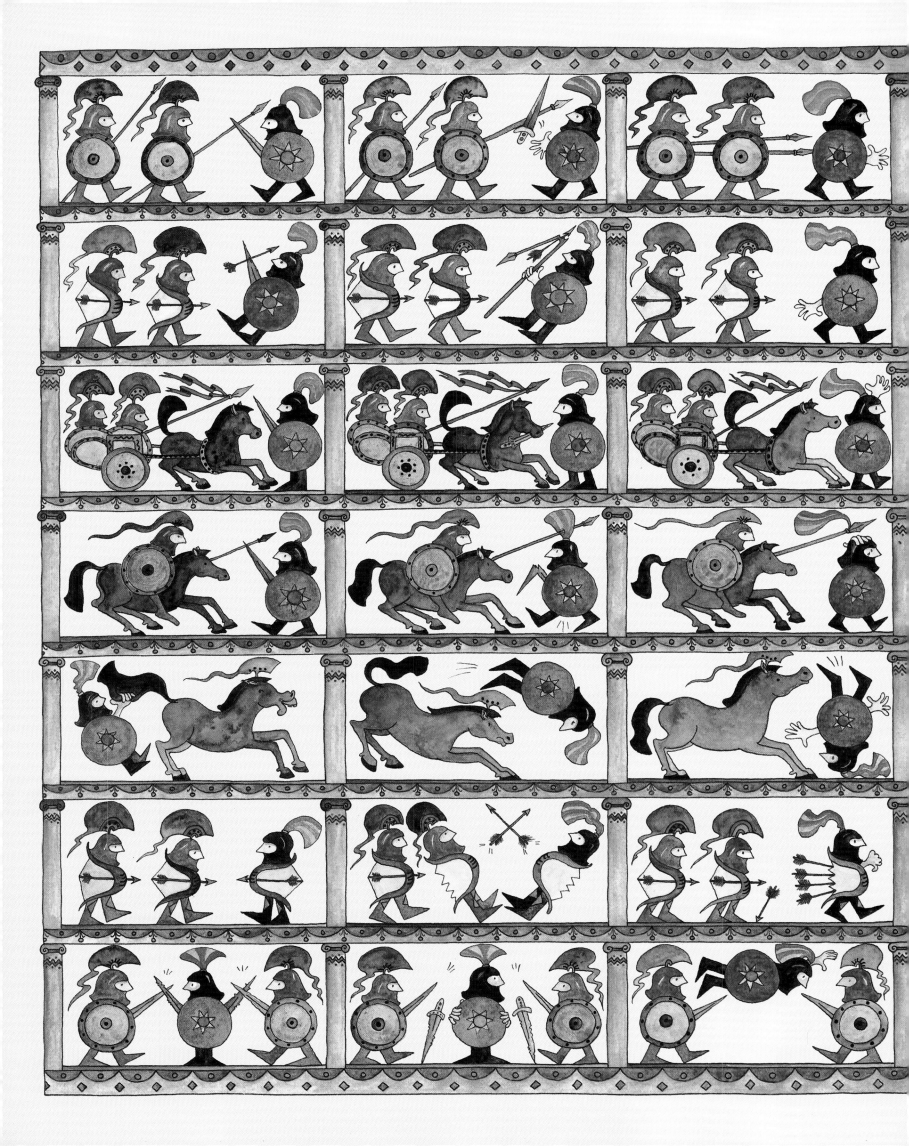